ORACLE BONES

Poems from the Time of Misrule

ORACLE BONES

Poems from the Time of Misrule

KEITH HOLYOAK

Goldfish Press
Seattle

Published by Goldfish Press

4545 42nd Avenue SW
Suite 211
Seattle, WA 98116

Manufactured in the United States of America

ISBN-13: 978-0-9787975-2-2
ISBN-10: 0-9787975-2-3

Photo of the author by Antoine Chesnais

Cover illustration by Jim Holyoak. Artist's rendering of a Hanzhong oracle bone. The inscribed characters (read top to bottom, right to left) literally translate as:

World how end?

This is world end way
Not is a bang but is a whimper

in memory of Heather Heyer (1985 – 2017)

martyr for social justice

"If you're not enraged, you're not paying attention."

Contents

Translator's Preface.............1

Oracle No.   *Page No.*
1.   Stone.....................7
2.   Jackals....................8
3.   Sparrows.................9
4.   Drums.....................10
5.   Propriety.................11
6.   Flood.................... 12
7.   Cicadas...................14
8.   Honor..................... 15
9.   Legs....................... 16
10.   Salt....................... 17
11.   Loyalty.................. 18
12.   Princelings.............. 19
13.   Homage..................20
14.   Taotie....................21
15.   Shapes.................... 22
16.   Pear.......................23
17.   Lips....................... 24
18.   Owl....................... 25
19.   Changes.................. 26
20.   Sunfall................... 27
21.   Gratitude.................28

Translator's Preface

I recall an old Chinese saying, "A journey of a thousand years carves a road with ten thousand twists." These translations represent one more twist on a symbolic journey that began millennia ago in central China when shamans engraved the earliest Chinese characters on animal bones. That long path intersected my far shorter one on a summer day in 2014, when I was visiting my wife's family in Hanzhong, a small city in Shaanxi province. Located roughly halfway between the larger and more famous cities of Xi'an and Chengdu, Hanzhong occupies a basin between mountain ranges. The Han River (the city's name means "center of the Han") runs through the town. The Han people have long been the dominant ethnic group in China, and this region was one of the cradles of early Chinese civilization, tracing back through the Han and Qin dynasties to yet earlier periods shrouded in mystery.

That afternoon I was taking a walk along the riverbank on the outskirts of town, when the footpath took a detour around a construction site in an area where new high-rise apartments were going up. As I passed beside an open pit in which a backhoe had recently been digging, I saw a group of workers gathered together, the machine left idle. Two of them knelt, each chipping away at a rock with hammer and chisel, while a third seemed to be diligently scrubbing some fragments with a brush. Off to the side two others were taking a break, knocking a plastic ball back and forth across a portable ping pong table. The rest smoked cigarettes and talked animatedly among themselves. One of the group noticed me standing at the perimeter, and pointed me out to his coworkers. Foreigners are still relatively rare in this area, especially one wandering alone far from the city center. The workers seemed to think I might have some interest in whatever the chiselers and the scrubber were doing, for several of them started laughing and gesturing for me to join them. I crossed the invisible line separating the path from the dig, and went over to take a closer look.

To my amazement, what I had thought were rock fragments were actually pieces of cracked bones, each carved with calligraphy. From my knowledge of Chinese prehistory, I surmised that the workers had uncovered a cache of oracle bones. Beginning around four millennia ago in the Shang dynasty[1], right at the edge of recorded Chinese history, animal bones (usually the shoulder bone of an ox, sometimes the shell of a turtle) were traditionally used in divination rituals. To foresee the future, a shaman would use the bones to perform a ritual of pyromancy. First, a question to the gods would be carved on the bone, typically relating to a pressing issue such as the prospects for a good harvest, the prognosis for a hunting expedition or a battle, or even the fate of the dynasty. Then a metal rod, heated to a high temperature, would be applied to the bone until it began to crack. The shaman's skill enabled him to interpret the pattern made by the cracks as the answer to his query. Finally, he would carve the message sent back by the gods onto the bone, so that question and answer formed a call and response.

Quite a number of the oracle bones had been cleaned and laid out in a row on the ground. The workers seemed very pleased when I expressed my admiration for their discovery. I was able to pull out my cellphone and take pictures of the inscriptions on several of the bones. I hinted that I would like to take one as a souvenir, but the apparent leader of the group shook his head. So, forced to be content with my photos, I

---

[1] Given the relatively southwestern location at which these particular bones were uncovered, it seems likely that they originated during the subsequent Western Zhou dynasty, which flourished about three thousand years ago.

waved goodbye and continued on my walk. The very next day, as previously arranged, I flew home to Los Angeles.

Back in my study, I scrutinized the photos more carefully. The images provided sufficient resolution to make most of the calligraphy legible.[2] After some reflection, I decided to make an effort to translate a few of the oracle bones. The archaic Chinese characters differ substantially from those in use today, posing problems likely to discourage many scholars. Fortunately, my command of ancient calligraphy is comparable to my fluency in reading modern Chinese, so I was able to proceed with the project without undue difficulty.

Here I present the results of my efforts to recreate in English the divinations preserved on the Hanzhong oracle bones. As I found these texts to be unusually poetic, I have attempted to convey not only what the messages say, but the manner in which they are expressed. For ease of reference I have given each a title, together with a number (written in the Shang-era script).[3] While staying as true to the original meaning as possible, I have of course been guided by the aim of rendering translations that may be appreciated by modern English readers. Written Chinese (especially in the ancient characters) is dense with meaning—much can be said in the small physical space of a bone. My English translations are considerably more expansive, sometimes using several words to explicate what the original conveyed with a single character. Though this increase in length might be considered a poetic loss, I believe the gain in intelligibility warrants it.

---

[2] The name of some unknown king was consistently omitted or scratched out on the oracle bones. I have marked these occurrences by [...].

[3] I simply assigned numbers to oracles in the order in which I happened to translate them.

I will leave it to the critics to assess the literary value of the oracle bones. Although the divinations are allusive, my own impression is that the set has a certain unity. It seems that these oracles were recorded during a time of misrule associated with some long-forgotten king. Foreshadowing symbolic devices that would characterize Chinese writing throughout the millennia to follow, the present political situation is often criticized obliquely by references to legends from the past. For example, the founder of his dynasty, Lord Tang (the Shang equivalent of George Washington) provides the prototype for the qualities of a virtuous ruler. In contrast, the last king of the preceding Xia Dynasty, named Jie, exemplifies a ruler whose selfish indulgence and caprice invites catastrophe. The divinations also express sentiments indirectly by referring to animals and plants that convey well-known symbolic meanings. These include mythological creatures such as the dragon (strong protector), the unicorn (wise and felicitous administration), the phoenix (beauty and honor), and the taotie (insatiable greed). Examples of real animals used to create metaphors include the sparrow (compassion), cicadas (rebirth) and the owl (whose call is an omen of death). The pear tree provides an emblem of justice, and the orchid embodies beauty and refinement. In addition to such specific symbols, the divinations refer to rituals of ancestor worship and to sacrifices designed to appease the gods of nature.

I am sorry to say I have no information about the disposition of the actual oracle bones. Though I harbor hope that at least some of them have found their way to reputable museums, they may well have been sold on the black market for Chinese antiquities. An even sadder fate befell many oracle bones uncovered in the nineteenth century—taken to be "dragon bones", many were ground into medicine used to treat malaria or heal wounds.

To my own embarrassment, I must confess that my digital photos of the bones were recently lost when the hard drive on my computer failed. (This is my punishment for failing to heed the admonition to create back-up copies of important files!) Fortunately, this accident happened after my translation project was essentially complete. For better or worse, these English versions of the ancient messages may well constitute a final twist in their long journey. Those of us who live during the epoch of the Later American Empire—a period of time scarcely longer than the decline and fall of China's final dynasty, the Qing—may find a few oracular nuggets engraved upon these bones.

Stone

A monument for our peerless King [...] what is to be engraved on the stone?

Worn away the moon climbs back to glory
A thousand thousand cycles
Change without change

The roofless palace overflows with moonlight
Recalls the fiery arrows
Rafters downrange

Moon-drenched this stone commands the royal courtyard
Last monument unfallen
Splendor turned strange

Its face under silver lichen smooth to the hand
No characters carved none lost
Change without change

Jackals

The thousand-year dynasty will it flourish?

Last of the dragon line cracks the sky
He roars where storm clouds swell
Look to the heavens and remember
Kingdoms rise and fall

Lord Tang is gone the dragons guard
The palace gates no more
Cry out cry out at what is lost
What claims the dragon's lair

The bloated tiger's orange mat
Breeds lice and stinks of mange
His teeth are corpses gums leak drool
Behold his power and cringe

On those he rules the tiger feeds
All innocence turned foul
The jackals lick his shriveled balls
And imitate his howl

Sparrows

How shall the dying counselor be honored?

A soldier he fell into the hands of the enemy
They beat him broke his limbs
He told them nothing

A noble he stood before the king and assembly
He could not raise his arms
His voice was steady

The Counselor said beware of false alliances
My Lord defend your people
He spoke his duty

Aged he died his king bestowed no favor
They laid him out for jackals
Left him unburied

The sparrows flocked each bore a bit of earth
Dropped it to build his grave mound
Wings dipped in mourning

Drums

The enemies of the great King [...] have they been eliminated?

Frost deepened riverbanks fell quiet
Days grew dim nights long
Inside their burrows alligators slept
Old songs were left unsung

Spring rains return hear thunder drum
Alligators wake
Their tails are thumping up and down the river
Voices answer back

Propriety

What rituals are to be observed?

Wild geese flock
They fly in formation
Above other birds
By night and by day

Their journey is long
Together they hasten
The leader they follow
Does not go astray

The stag seeks to breed
The doe that he sired
Along with the others
A daughter desired

Beasts have their ways
The gods cast no blame
Man gets to choose
His path and his name

Flood

Why does the river spill its banks for so long?

The people thirsted
Lord Tang stood up his pyre was lit
He prayed accept my body freely offered
The gods were pleased rains fell
The fire was doused
The people long remember
Lord Tang

Spring came and went
The rituals were not observed
No lamb was offered oracles unsought
The river god grew angry
His waters rose
The people cried remember
Lord Tang

Snows melt again
The rituals were not observed
No ox was offered silence at the palace
The river god enraged
Unsheathes his waters
The people cry remember
Lord Tang

The moon is now auspicious
Bring forth the princess from her chamber
Bind her float her on a bamboo raft
Bride of the river god
His waters sated
May people long remember
Lady Li

✝

Cicadas

What has become of the rival clans that the great King [...]
defeated?

Gone the traitors broken
Those who would not prostrate themselves
Were thrust down into the earth
Became the bark of trees
Silent as fungus

Silent as cicadas
Gripping tree roots shed torn skin
Red wings mark time for rebirth
Shrill tymbal clicks crescendo
Sounding among us

)(

Honor

Is the time propitious for attaining a high position in the royal court?

In the time of Lord Tang
Most sage and benevolent ruler
Wealth and honor bestowed on the worthy
Exalted their name

In the time of King Jie
Caprice makes iniquity crueler
Wealth and honor bestowed on the henchmen
Casts light on their shame

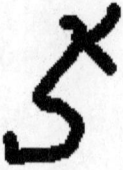

Legs

How may the king unite the people?

Those of the north will ride all day
Then sleep beneath the stars
They drink too much they tell no lies
Trust them to win our wars

Those of the south will dress in silk
The ladies of the court
They eat too well they laugh at fools
Trust them to make our art

Lord Tang bestrode the north and south
He held his people close
The ruler who has lost one leg
Will soon have lost them both

Salt

How can the royal family profit though the people be poor?

A man needs light
To grow his crops to find his way
The sun bathes all
And no one pays for light

A man needs water
To slake his thirst to cool his brow
The rains drench all
And no one pays for water

A man needs air
To fill his lungs to heat his blood
The winds blow free
And no one pays for air

A man needs salt
To drive his heart to fire his brain
Seize all the mines
And make men pay for salt

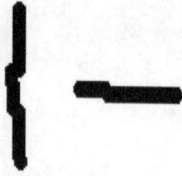

Loyalty

*In the reign of the great King [...] what deed brings greatest honor
to the realm?*

The decree was sent down
To garrisons along the border
Seize the migrants
Kill the men
Rip the infant from its mother
Enslave the women

Babe at her breast
Clad in wool rags she crossed the border
A soldier loomed
His blade raised high
The loyal guard recalled the order
Waved her on by

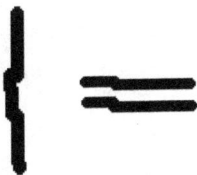

Princelings

Will the sons of the great King [...] maintain the glory of the dynasty?

As dragons beget dragons
So serpents beget serpents

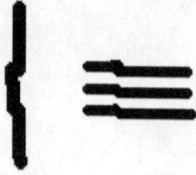

Homage

Should the illustrious King [...] make offerings to the royal ancestors?

Let those who drink water
Remember those who dug the well
Lay food upon the altar
Bow low in the ancestral hall

The kings who came before
Paid homage kept their line unbroken
Through times of peace and war
Sons of Lord Tang are not forgotten

The last king of his line
Will not be praised on standing stones
Nor will his name be seen
By those who read the oracle bones

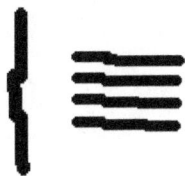

Taotie

What image should be cast on the bronze cauldron to be set at the palace gate?

The Beast of Greed is formless
Its jaws gape beyond the heavens
It has no purpose but one
Its eyes seek meat its tusks impale
Its claws rend flesh its teeth grind bone

The Beast of Greed is boundless
The earth can never fill its belly
It has no purpose but one
It feasts on men consumes itself
Gobbles the sun devours the moon

Let those who enter through this gate
Give thought that others need to eat

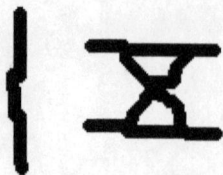

Shapes

What fate does the diviner foresee?

My path comes to an end
Covered by rising water
Beneath a hanging pine
I sit me down and ponder
Shapes drift in the fog
Most pass away some linger

Pear

When will the phoenix fly again in the kingdom?

The beaters flushed the dragon horse
Out of the forest
The princelings with their ivory bows
Brought it down
Those who feast on unicorn
Are surely cursed
He who drinks its blood
Will die alone

The north star fixed guides lesser stars
They turn toward it
The pear tree shaded the Duke of Zhou
He judged all fairly
Power cut loose from duty
Turns mean and sordid
The axman followed orders
Felled the pear tree

Bereft of pear and unicorn
The phoenix leaves the land forlorn

{ †

Lips

Who is to be trusted?

Close your ears to sycophants
Their tongues turn good to evil
They love to praise what should be hated

Pay no heed to sorcerers
Who make rich villains victims
Of crimes their victims perpetrated

Judge this water hot or cold
Slaves' lips cannot be trusted
Ignore them raise your cup and taste it

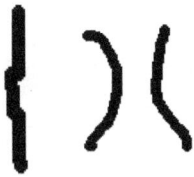

Owl

Will the great King [...] be blessed with sleep tonight?

The moon rises after the midnight bell
The demon has swallowed a little more
Things are eroding enemies close in
The gods will choose the time for war

Your concubines no longer bring you joy
Affections bend as does the willow
Why did you plant that other tree so near
You knew the mulberry rhymes with sorrow

The jackals guarding the palace slip away
One of them swears he heard the owl
Cry on each stroke of the midnight gong
Someone who sleeps will lose their soul

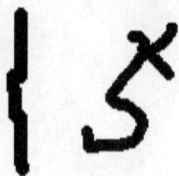

15

Changes

Is the king well served by his ministers?

Study the past the future is written there
Fools enjoy their careless pleasure
King Jie drank wine riding astride his chancellor
Kept him on a golden tether
Whinnying to praise his master

The age is disordered wisdom beaten down
Orchid and iris have lost their fragrance
The glutton for power goes blind as he grows reckless
At last ensnared in his own rages
He drowns beneath a flood of changes

Sunfall

Will the Mandate of Heaven remain with our illustrious sovereign?

In a lake of wine naked men and women
Drank as they swam to service
The king on his island

Before the axe came down the counselor said
Our enemies rejoice
They call you tyrant

King Jie laughed who dares disturb the sun
Until the sun burns out
This earth is my land

The people cried oh sun when will you perish
Better to scream in rage
Than cower silent

His concubine dreamed a greater sun arose
Hurled the old one earthward
Shrunken its fire spent

The unicorn returns and now the phoenix
Perched on a sapling pear tree
Takes flight defiant

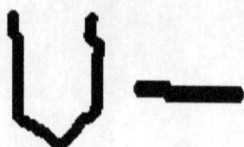

Gratitude

How will the peerless King [...] reward the diviner who reads the admonitions of the gods?[*]

---

[*] For some unknown reason, no response was recorded on this final oracle bone.

28

Also by Keith Holyoak

The Spider's Thread: Metaphor in Mind, Brain, and Poetry
(MIT Press, 2019)

The Gospel According to Judas
(Dos Madres Press, 2015)

Foreigner: New English Poems in Chinese Old Style
(Dos Madres Press, 2012)

My Minotaur: Selected Poems 1998-2006
(Dos Madres Press, 2010)

Facing the Moon: Poems of Li Bai and Du Fu
(Oyster River Press, 2007)

www.ingramcontent.com/pod-product-compliance
Lightning Source LLC
Chambersburg PA
CBHW021149020426
42331CB00005B/963